D1581493

PIG IN THE PARLOUR

Northern Ireland in Black and White

by ROWEL FRIERS

*'The more I think of politicians,
the less I think of them.'*

BLACKSTAFF PRESS

BELFAST

1972

© ROWEL FRIERS 1972

Published by

BLACKSTAFF PRESS LIMITED

84 Wandsworth Road

Belfast BT4 3LW

SBN 85640 012 2

Printed in Northern Ireland by the Northern Whig Ltd, 6 Bridge Street, Belfast.

To

A Long Suffering Public

INTRODUCTION

I have never been able to rationalise my passion for cartoons. Whether it be Tom and Jerry on the screen, or Flook, Fred Basset, the Wizard of Id and dozens of others in the newspapers, I swallow them all with avid relish and a total absence of discrimination. I have to admit that I often do so with a slight feeling of guilt, an uncomfortable sensation that it is a rather childish enthusiasm. But then I come across some intellectual giant and discover that he is just as bad a cartoon nut as I am and my mental virility is restored.

Rowel Friers is very high on my list of favourite cartoonists – indeed, he has been for as long as I can remember. From time to time there have been professional dealings between us, but my first contact with him can best be described as amateur, or at best, semi-professional. Because I was a journalist and also a keen follower of cricket the Irish Cricket Union decided in 1958 that I was best qualified to produce a brochure to mark the centenary game in Dublin between Ireland and the MCC. It was a shoe-string job with a vengeance. Apart from the Union's undertaking to pay the printing costs (big deal!) the only other expenses available to me amounted to a fiver.

As every fool knows, any once-only publication is largely sold on its cover and it was clear to me that Rowel Friers was the man to sell this particularly difficult product. But how does one approach an Academician of the Royal Ulster Academy and expect him to undertake such a frivolous project for five quid? The answer is simple. You phone the Great Man, explain your difficulty and get the goods almost by return of post. Cricket is a solemn game. Friers is not solemn. His cover drawing was a hilarious and totally irreverent caricature of the noble W G Grace. It was described by one ancient Ulster cricketer as 'not very nice'. But the kids loved it, bought it and the Cricket Union made a very handsome profit on the brochure.

Apart from the fact that this was a classic con-job perpetrated on a good-natured artist, it was also the first indication I had of the nature of the beast. I reached the tentative conclusion that Friers was no great respecter of convention *per se* and was also a little mad. Subsequent encounters caused me to modify this early impression — the man has not the slightest respect for convention and is totally mad in a very sane way. Convention and so-called sanity are what have brought this wee island of ours into conflict and misery.

Rowel has the marvellous and almost unique (in Ireland) combination of qualities of wit and self-criticism, together with the ability to life his sights above the political madness that blinds normal vision and enables him to focus on the foibles, the posturings and the downright moral dishonesty of those who nightly parade themselves on the telly. He is not so much a clown (though a lot of his work has a clownish quality), as a deflater and a pin-pricker of inflated egos. He is almost wicked in his sense of direction when he selects a target and yet he is so gentle in the way he makes fun of it.

It may not be an over-statement to say that Rowel Friers and Jimmy Young might end up in the social history of Northern Ireland, because they could both derive laughs from material which, to comfortable outsiders like myself in Dublin, seems totally tragic and obscene. This is the ultimate test of pure satire, the portrait of an artist as a human being whose involvement in the sheer awfulness of day-to-day life has in no way diminished his sense of the ridiculous.

Conor J O'Brien

ACKNOWLEDGEMENTS

The cartoons in this book originally appeared in the following publications :-
Belfast Telegraph, Daily Express, Dublin Opinion, Fortnight, Punch, and the *Sunday Independent.*

GENERAL COMMENT

'Buenos Dias, Pancho - You would theenk we were in Ulster!'

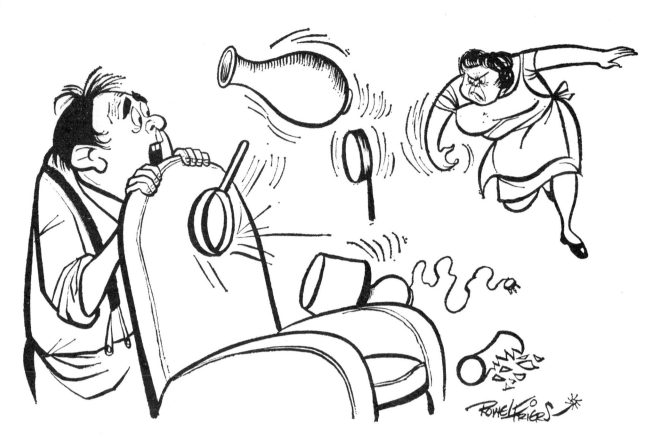

'Who the ..... do you think you are — Mary Peters?'

'We hired a second set and watched it on both channels.'

'No space, unhealthy conditions — It's ridikilis the way they keep them animals at Bellevue.'

'Hey, Mary, do you remember did we have any
tall black and white wans before the cold spell.'

'Madam, that is not funny!'

'Would you have a garden chair I could borrow?'

'Which one of yiz was whinin' to the boss about the steak?'

'Somebody told him "I am curious Yellow" is the Late Night Movie.'

'A guy can't think of EVERYTHING!'

'I see the Maguire boys are home for Christmas.'

'Quick — follow that horseman!'

'My gay, my dashing Romeo, my cup of loving wine,
Come run with me, come fly away, and be my Valentine.'

'Next, please.'   Reproduced by permission of Punch

'You're a very fortunate man—I happen to be a doctor.'

'Doctor, I forgot to tell you—the pain only affects me when I lie down like this.'

'Thon wuz only a frienly

k starts the seezin prapar.'

'.....and one last word!'

'Someone has fainted!'

'Leaves me with sixteen yards
to make up! And if I win he
gets a medal too!'

'Heavens! I've forgotten
to use the pole!'

'No thanks, I'm driving!'

23

ROWEL FRIGGS

'Daddy knows best, dear, and daddy says he's not out!'

'I hate to have to tell you this, boys, but your share of the gross takings won't warrant more than a nice gentlemanly brawl.'

LEFT HAND DRIVE

'We've discovered we get better results when he shoots and I retrieve.'

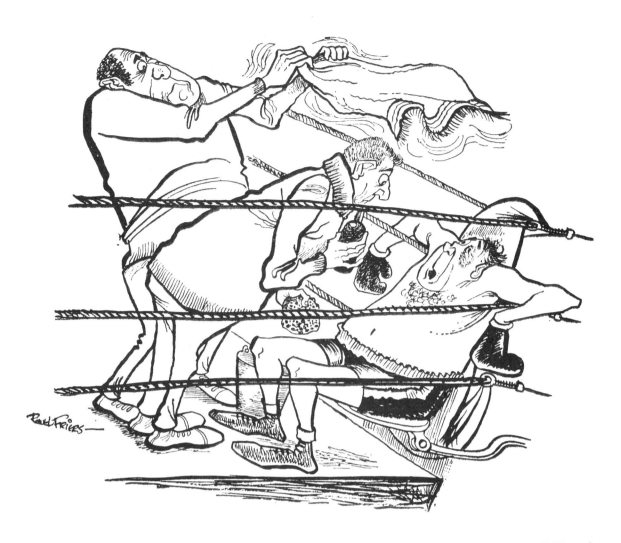

'There was a period during that last round when I could have sworn I was in Donegall Place.'

'Now, THERE'S health for you!'

'Gentlemen, I warn you, if we can't have a clean
open game—I'll get TOUGH with you!'

'Like this, stupid!'

'Easy on with the jerseys, boys. They've gone up to
£2.50!'

'I'm feeling a little out of form.'

'I wish she wouldn't keep getting this elevator attendant.'

'Tryin' to make a cod of me, eh?'

28

'Hey, it's illegal to fish here!'

Reproduced by permission of Punch

'They say the better-known public schools are
even harder to get into.'

'There's a fly in it!'

29

'To quote the explanatory memorandum, its objects are: "To replace the present separate codes by one co-ordinated scheme of Social Insurance; to extend the present scope of social insurance by bringing an increased number of persons within its ambit; to provide higher benefits than those payable now under the present codes and to introduce new benefits." Unquote.'

'And what, can you tell me, does the likes of yer man St Laurent know about dressin' the likes of you or me?'

'Twist must be mad – this stuff stinks!'

'No, no, Prince! Over here, boy! Over here!'

'Let him poke me once more in the flank — just once more!'

'I can't afford a coat with wool at the price it is.'

'Yum, Yum! Phosphates!'

'Wouldn't they be sore if they knew we hadn't a plate of glass after all?'

'When they said "Neck-tie Party" I presumed it would be a formal affair.'

'Fire!'

'It's always the same when anyone leaves my most comfortable chair.'

'There must be some mistake — this is a Valentine card!'

'At what time do you expect your
mother back, Johnny!'

33

'I see someone has been putting a little bit away for a rainy day!'

'O K boys. You know the drill. The councillor with the polka dot tie.'

'Yes, I had a card from the Missus. She returns to-night—she says she'll be glad to get home!'

'Quickly, Bootle — my glasses.'

'And you tell me, Lieutenant, that your parachute failed to open until ten feet from the ground.'

'They'll be mad when they dis

'idn't manage to get a turkey.'

'Between thon dirty great glowery cloud an' thon greenish grey one an' behind thon mustard mist is one of the nicest landscapes in Ulster!'

'I told you not to row too far from the pier!'

'And I came out here to get away from squawking kids!'

Sea-saw By Rowel Friers

'Oh, by the way, did you get that Widows and Orphans Welfare Scheme through all right before we left?'

'Well, I'd rather be on sentry-go than eat yon pudding!'

'Author! Author!'

'Maybe I do look like
an owl, but how do
you look yourself?'

'Are you sure you belong to the right
union?'

The FRIERS Book of Records

(under the influence of GUINNESS)

Quentin Quench who drank 16 rounds of whiskey without standing a round himself

John Mutt who worked for the same firm for 50 years and never got a gold watch.

Willie Nitt scored a record 26 goals in two months—all against his own side.

Mrs. Cynthia Menace has been driving a car for 35 years and has never had a hard word to say about men drivers

Sean O'Pochle has been an M.P. for 40 years and has never once contradicted himself

Miss Hilary Bustle efficiency expert started 5 years ago with **LYMP** industries (500 employees) Now runs the entire business single handed

43

'I always think that Clancy is too direct in his approach to make a good canvasser.'

'I think the Corporation are trying to sell us the buses on Hire Purchase.'

'Sure wadda ya want till go till the Ideel Home fawr — havint we wun here?'

'Can you see yourself as Santa Claus?'

'It's about your Mr Santa Claus.'

'The Duke says if you leave a pick of that turkey he'll never forgive you.'

The Wicked Uncle

'From this attitude I can only conclude you don't believe in me.'

'Lizzie – what resolutions did I make last night?'

'I'll drown his shamrock!'

HERE WAS THE NEWS

'If you're Irish come into the parlour.....'

IRELAND UNITED

KNOTTY PROBLEM

Horatio Lynch — 'I see nothing.'

ULSTER '71
With acknowledgments to Thinkers everywhere

HARVEST '71

'What I'd like to know is — who's brainwashing who?'

'Ivery time I hear them politicians on the telly I think it's a recorded repeat.'

27 November 1971

11 December 1972

'Sorry, Guv, we can't mike exceptions!'

'Dear Mr Faulkner, owing to prevailing climatic conditions, I regret...'

18 December 1972

'Hands up all you who will be stayin' for Christmas dinner.'

8 January 1972

'They could have named it "Call My Bluff" or even "Degeneration Game"!'

15 January 1972

'You take yer life in yer hans in town these days — thon winter sales is despirt.'

'..... 68, 42, 91, 74 come in your time's NOT up'

29 January 1972

'When you're at it fellas — clean the plugs and check the oil.'

THE GRAND SLALOM

5 February 1972

Rowel Friers

presents his screen awards

Brian Faulkner for
his role as
"Little Big Man"

Phelim O'Neill
as
"The Go-Between"

Jack Lynch
for
"This Weak"

Hume & Currie
as
"The Comedians"

Bernadette
for
"Talkback"

and Sammy Snout
wins the Best
Supporting Role

Suggestion for a panel of experts on Northern Ireland affairs

4 March 1972

ON THE HOT AIR

From right — Paul McCartney, Senator Edward Kennedy, Vanessa Redgrave, John Lennon, Yoko and and a Resident Authority.

Song of Bernadette

18 March 1972

AIR FRANCE

The last time I saw Paris.

THE

RSHAL

O! My offense is rank,
it smells to heaven;
It hath the primal eldest curse upon't,
A brother's murder

—Hamlet

THE WRITING ON THE WALL   8 April 1972

25 March 1972

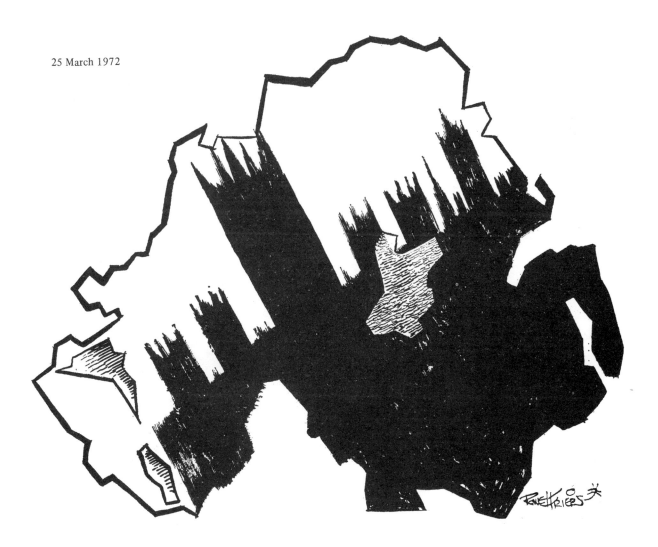

'What I say is — forget tribunals, bring in Clint Eastwood.'

Know summthin? — I believe I've forgotten how to fly.

'Tighter rein, tighter rein'

'Who can be wise, amaz'd, temperate and furious, loyal and neutral, in a moment? No man'

– Macbeth

'I hate till be alarmist Wullie but it luks like yer missus has declared a no-go area.'

27 May 1972

'Will he only behave himself if we do EVERYTHING he wants?'

'Good heavens! I didn't realise our hospital food was
that good.'

'Rude am I in my speech, and little blessed with the soft phrase
of peace' – Othello (or Sean MacStiofain)

'He wudn't have tha nerve — bline drunk an'
a lamp post walked in till 'im.'

BIRD IN THE HAND

GETTING AWAY FROM IT ALL IN ENGLAND

10 July 1971

Rowel Friers in a go-go area

15 July 1972

'What's the next move?'

19 August 1972

'What do ye say tae a plebiscite on the border, Wullie John?'
'Ach, so long as ats no wan o' thon skyscraper blawks!'.

12 August 1972

'*The umbrella is successfully re-erected, I think. I am the man holding it up.*' — Mr William
Craig, leader of Vanguard, interviewed on BBC Radio.

30 September 1972

23 September 1972

'I think they're trying to make a monkey out of me.'

Harvest '72